Adult Coloring Book:

20 Stress Relieving Landscapes And Amazing Animal Patterns

Katherine Kennedy & Mary Hoffman

© 2015

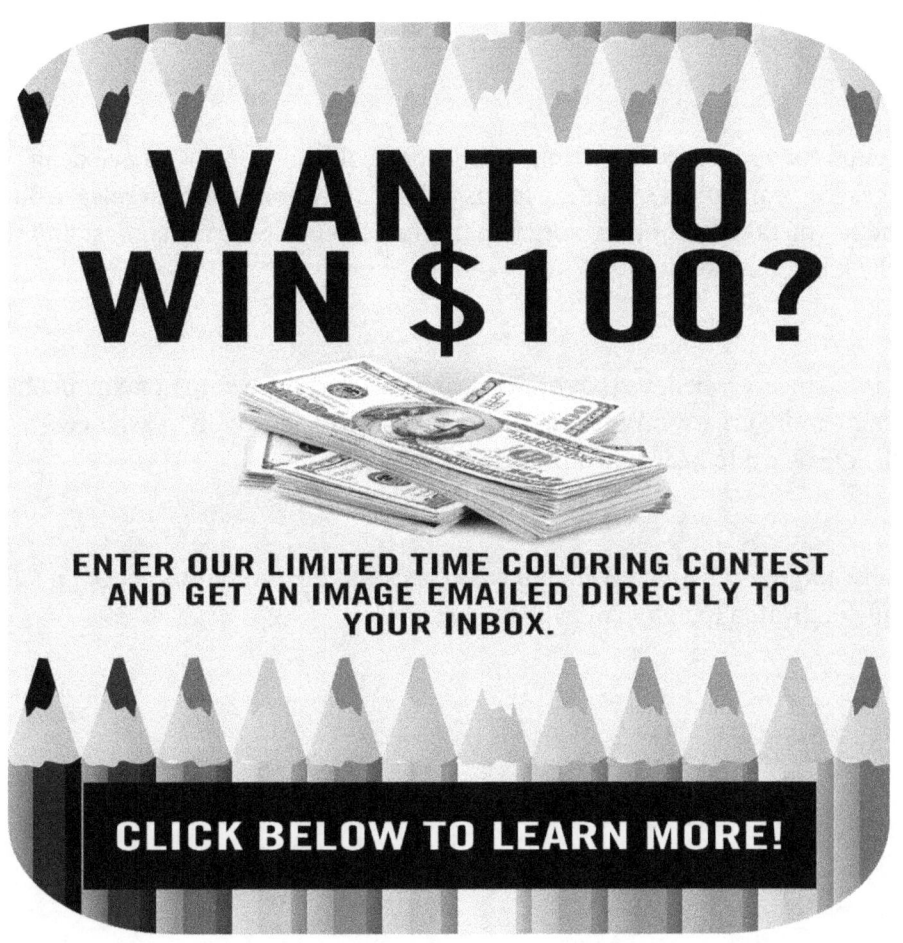

TYPE IN THE LINK BELOW TO ENTER THE CONTEST NOW!

>>>>>https://zenithpublishing.leadpages.co/adult-colouring-books/<<<<<<<<

Greeting fellow artists:

We're very excited for you check out our first published coloring book. We have been creating coloring images for years and it's exciting for us to have the opportunity to release our work the public. We hope you take the opportunity to participate in our coloring contest and we wish you the best of the luck.

Over the years we sincerely believe that our coloring patterns have helped many people reduce stress and become more creative. We hope that our work will allow you to achieve similar feelings. We look forward to hearing your feedback.

If we want to learn more about us and what we do please check out our "About Us" page on our website, which is totally dedicated to adult coloring books:

http://bestadultcoloringbooks.com/about/

Sincerely,

Katherine & Mary

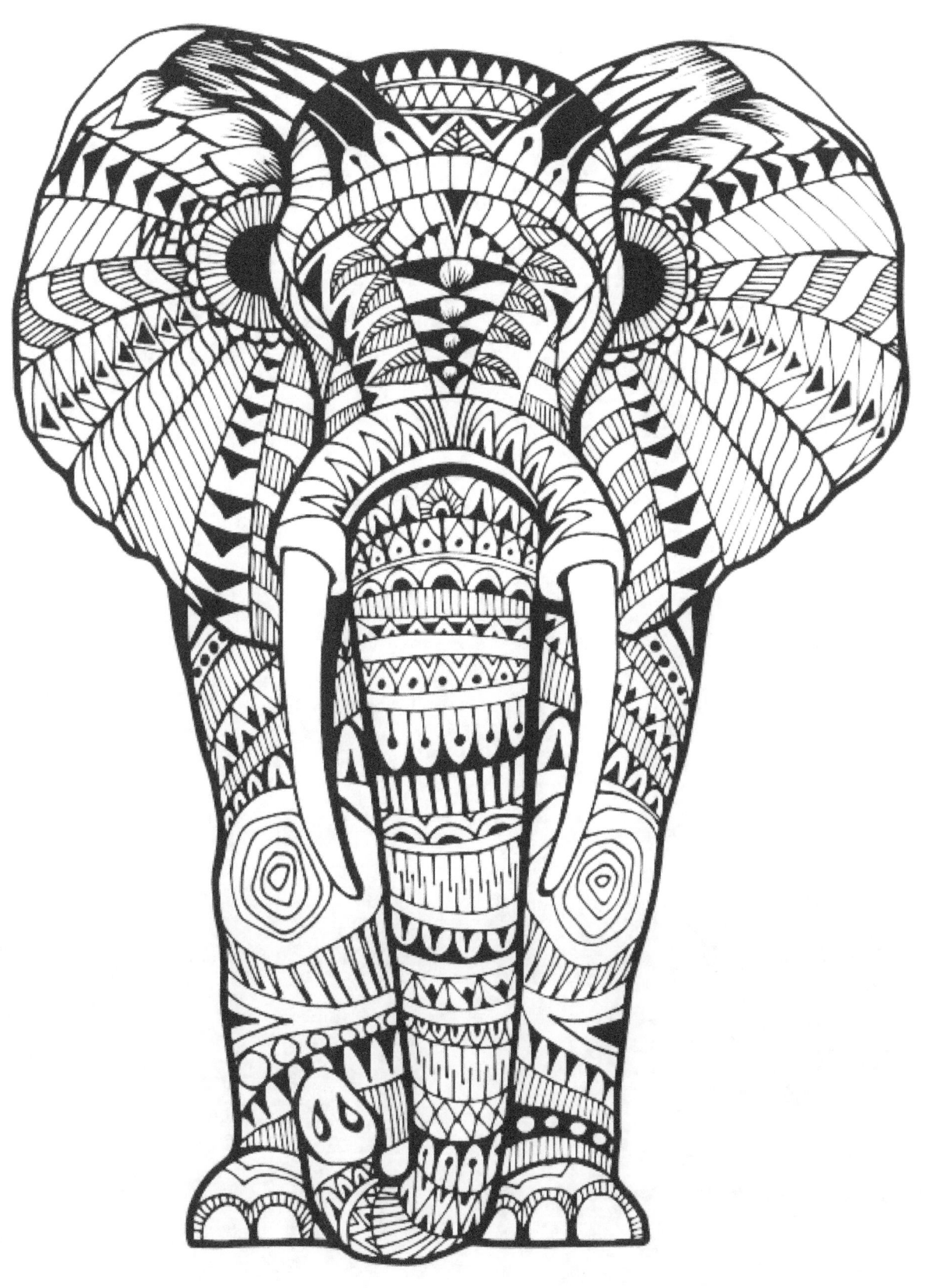

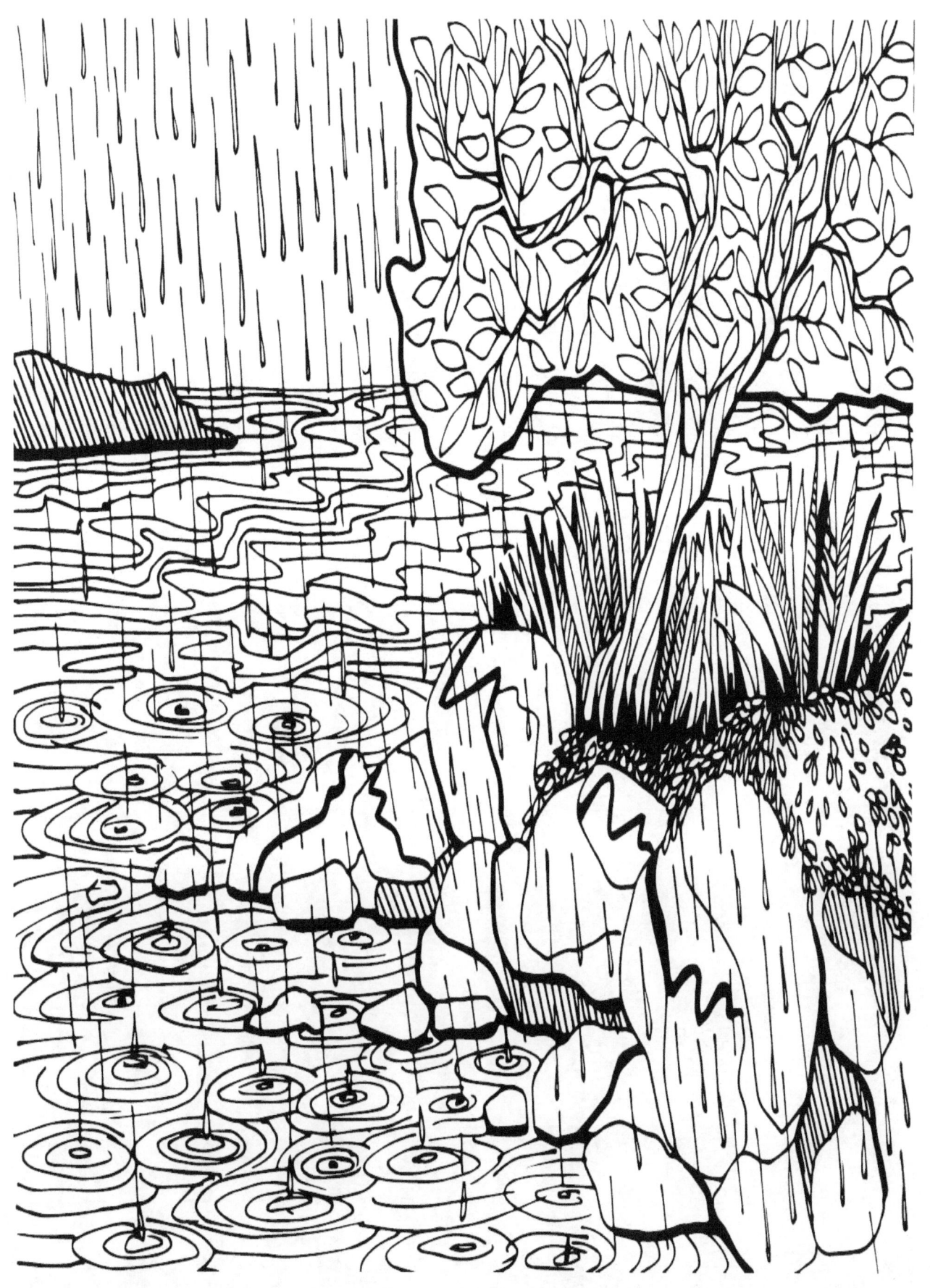

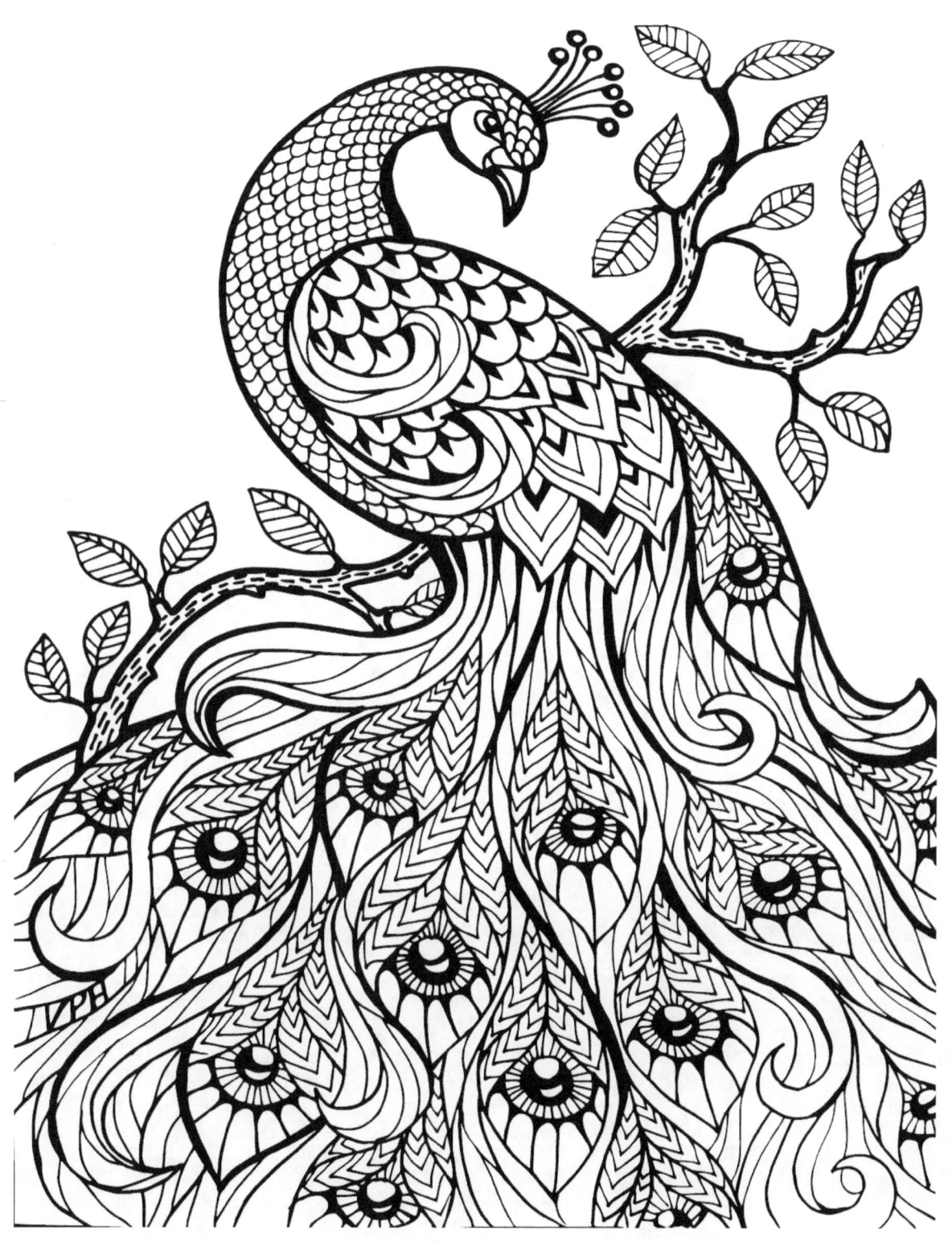

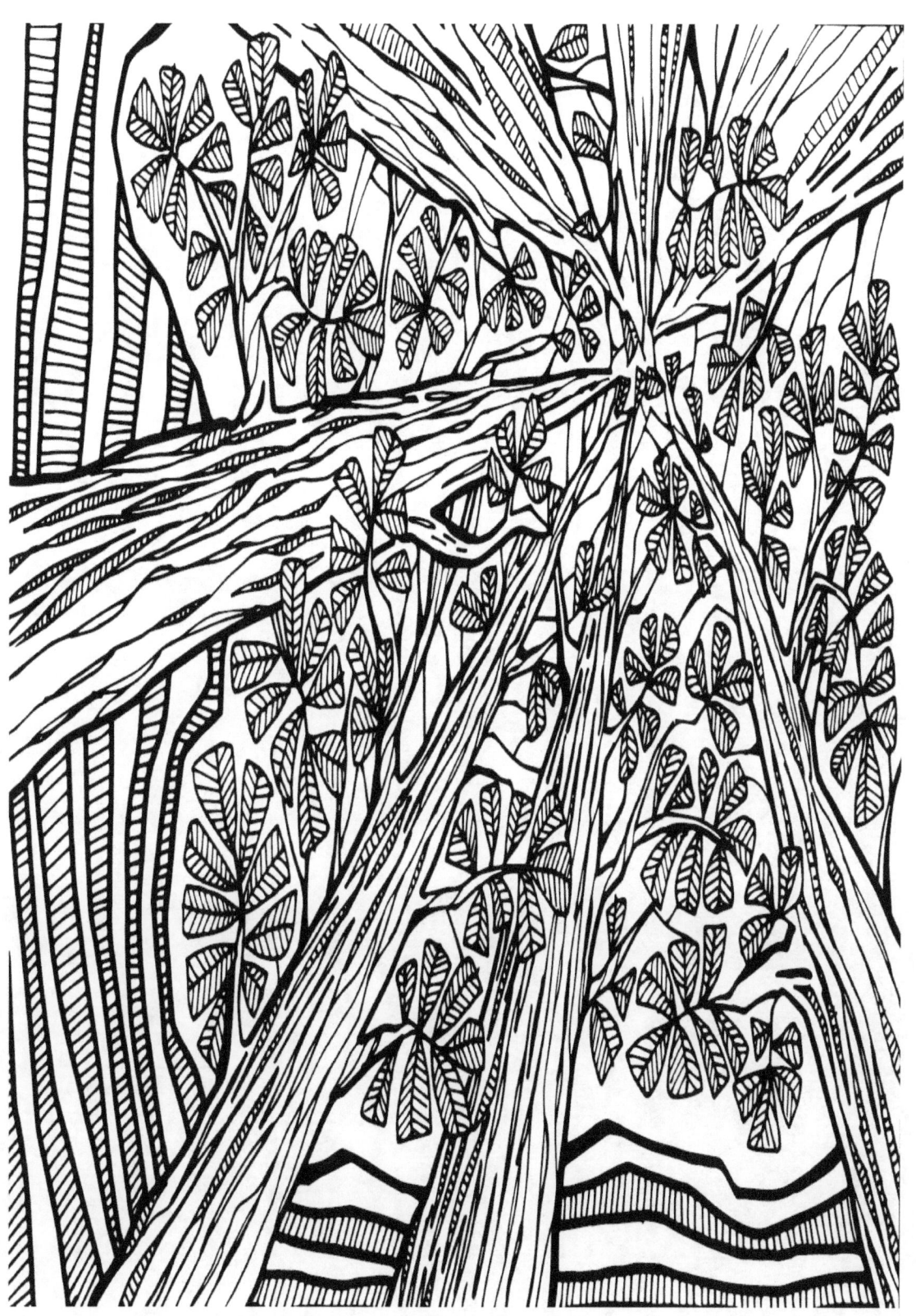

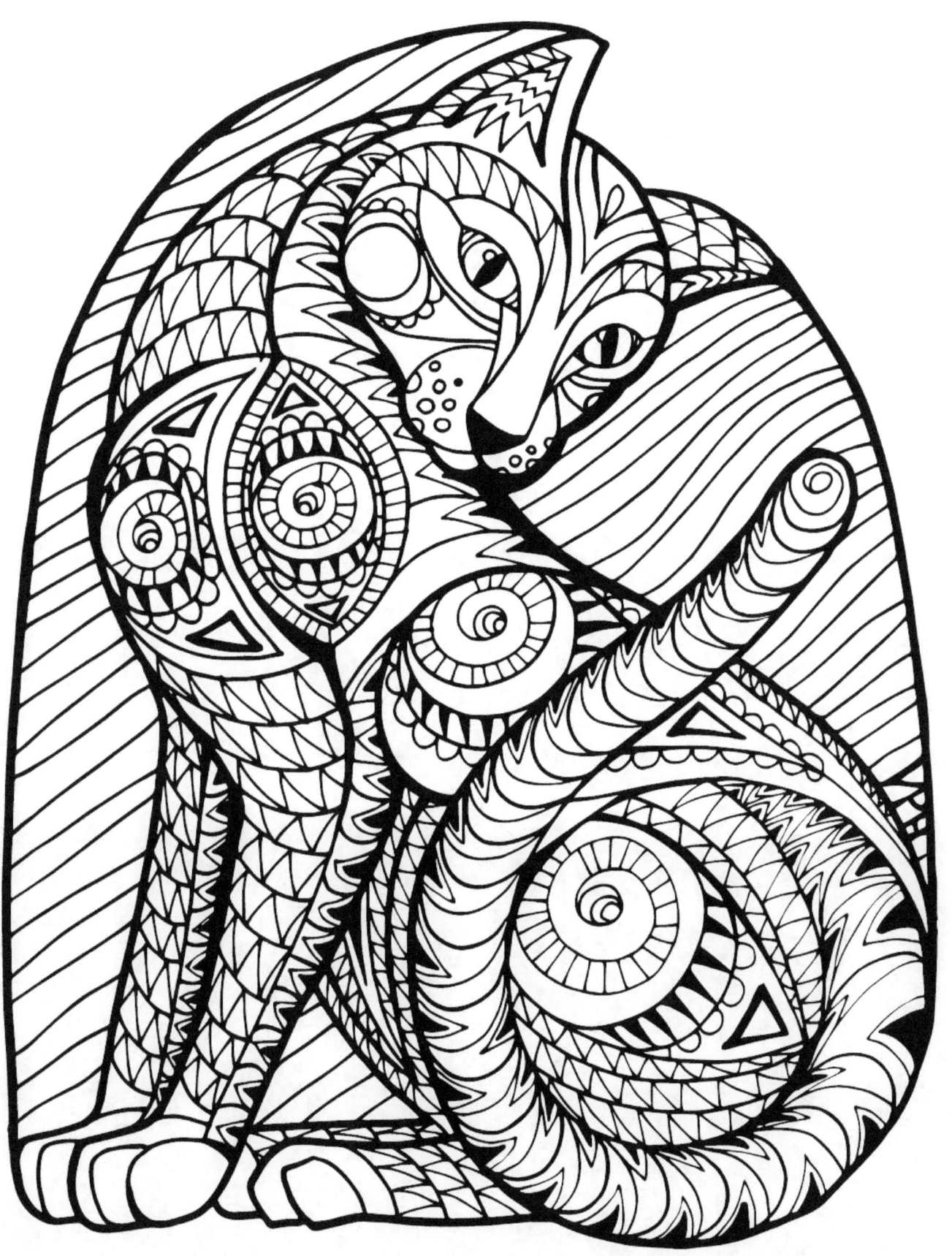

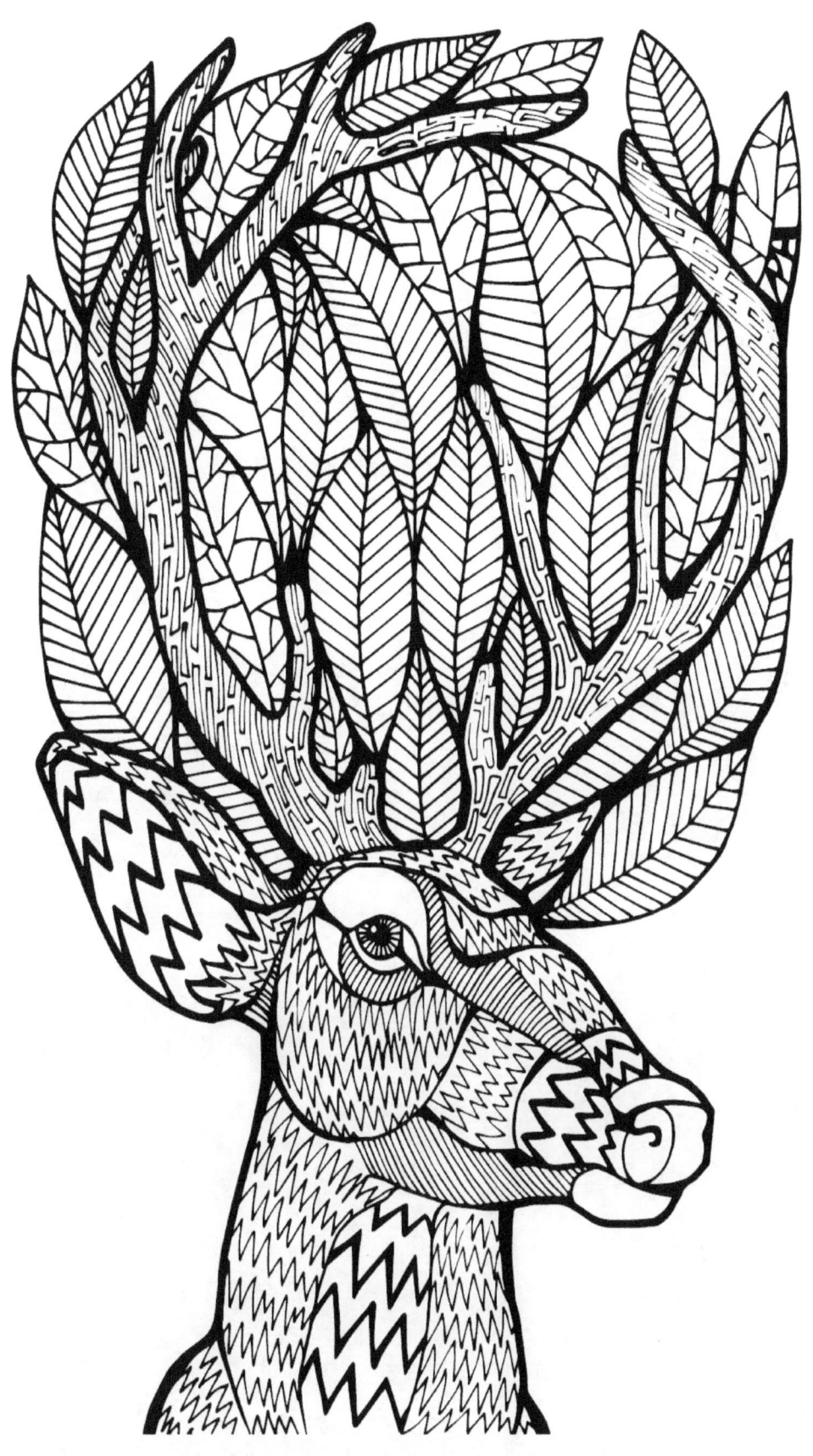

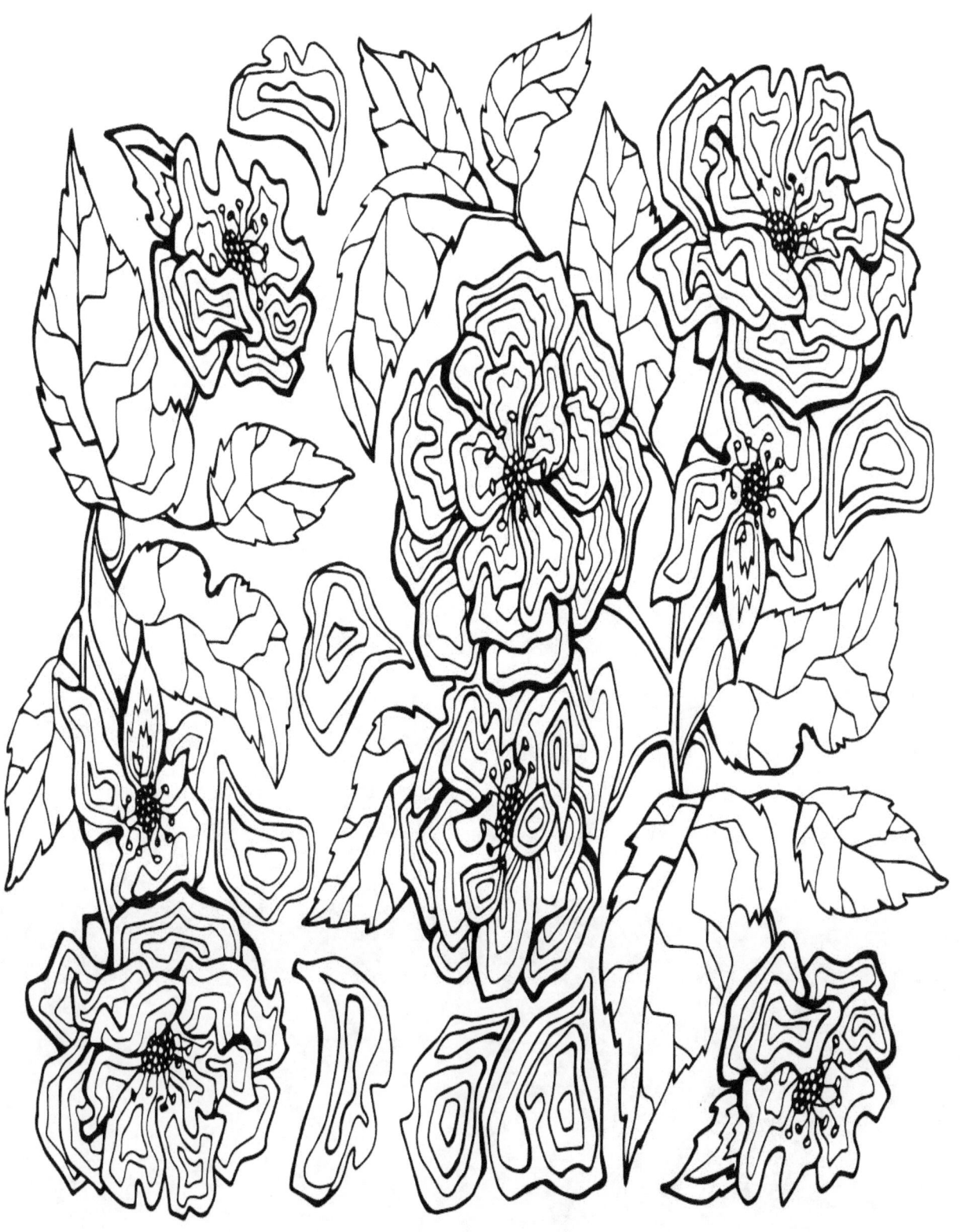

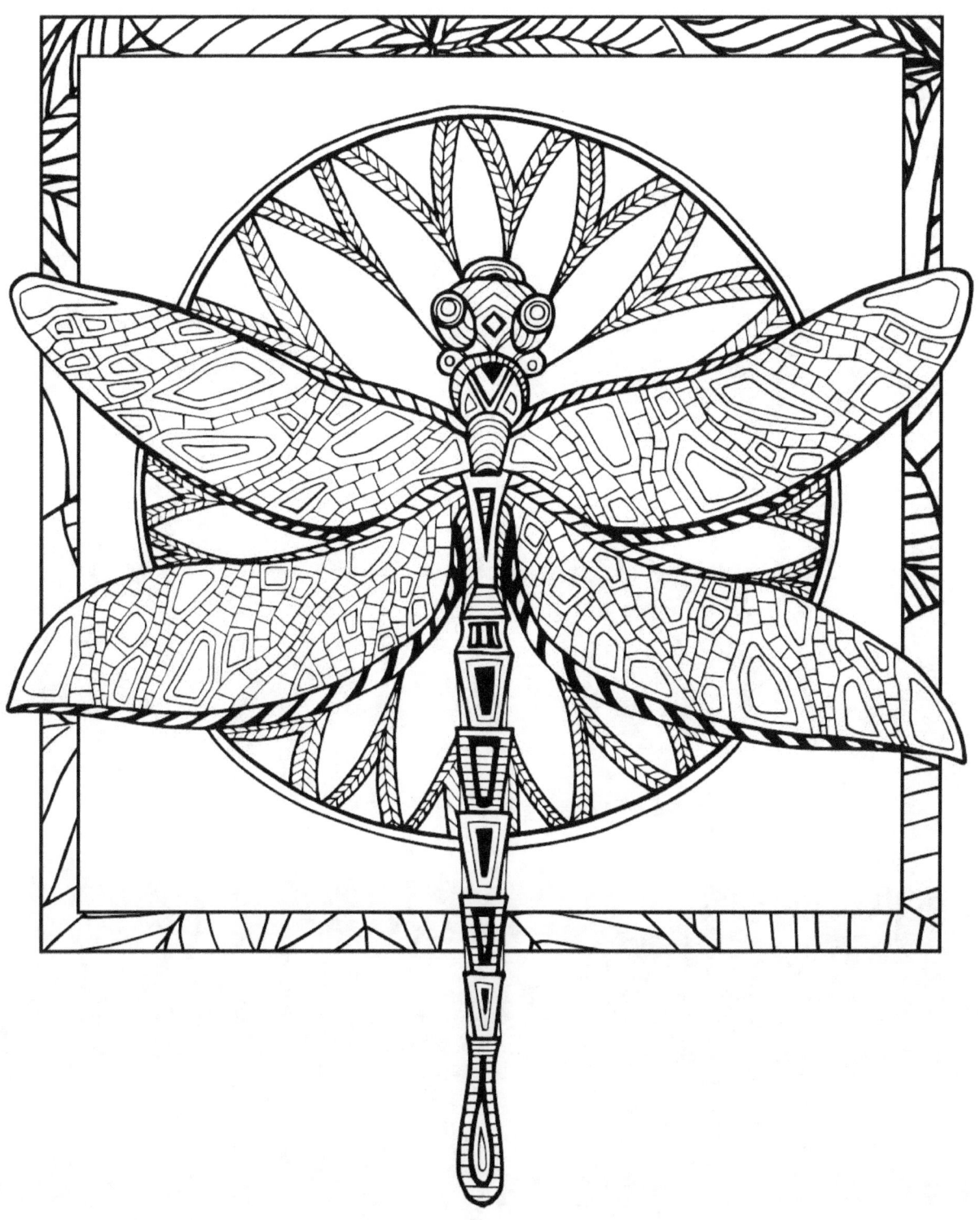

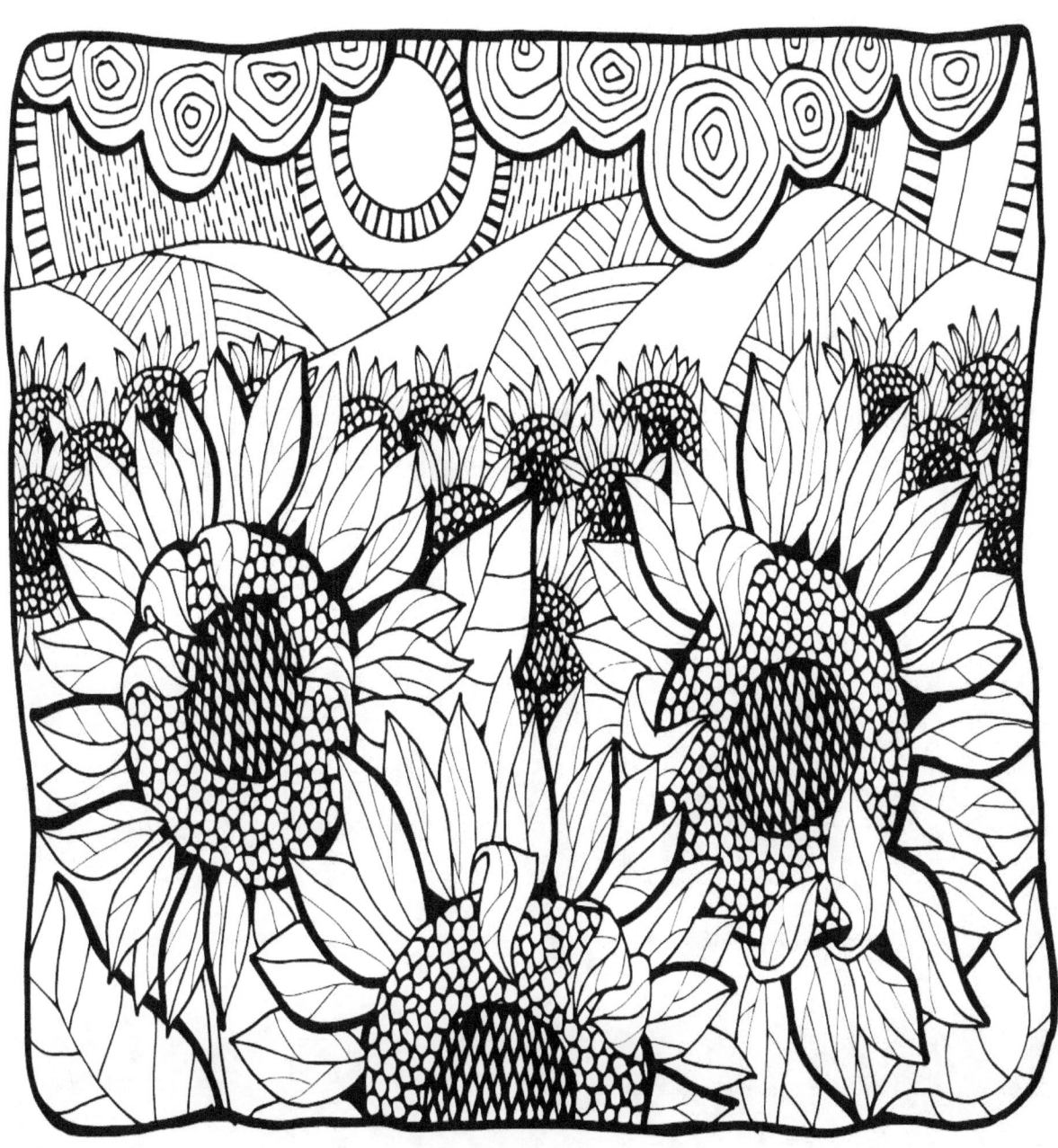

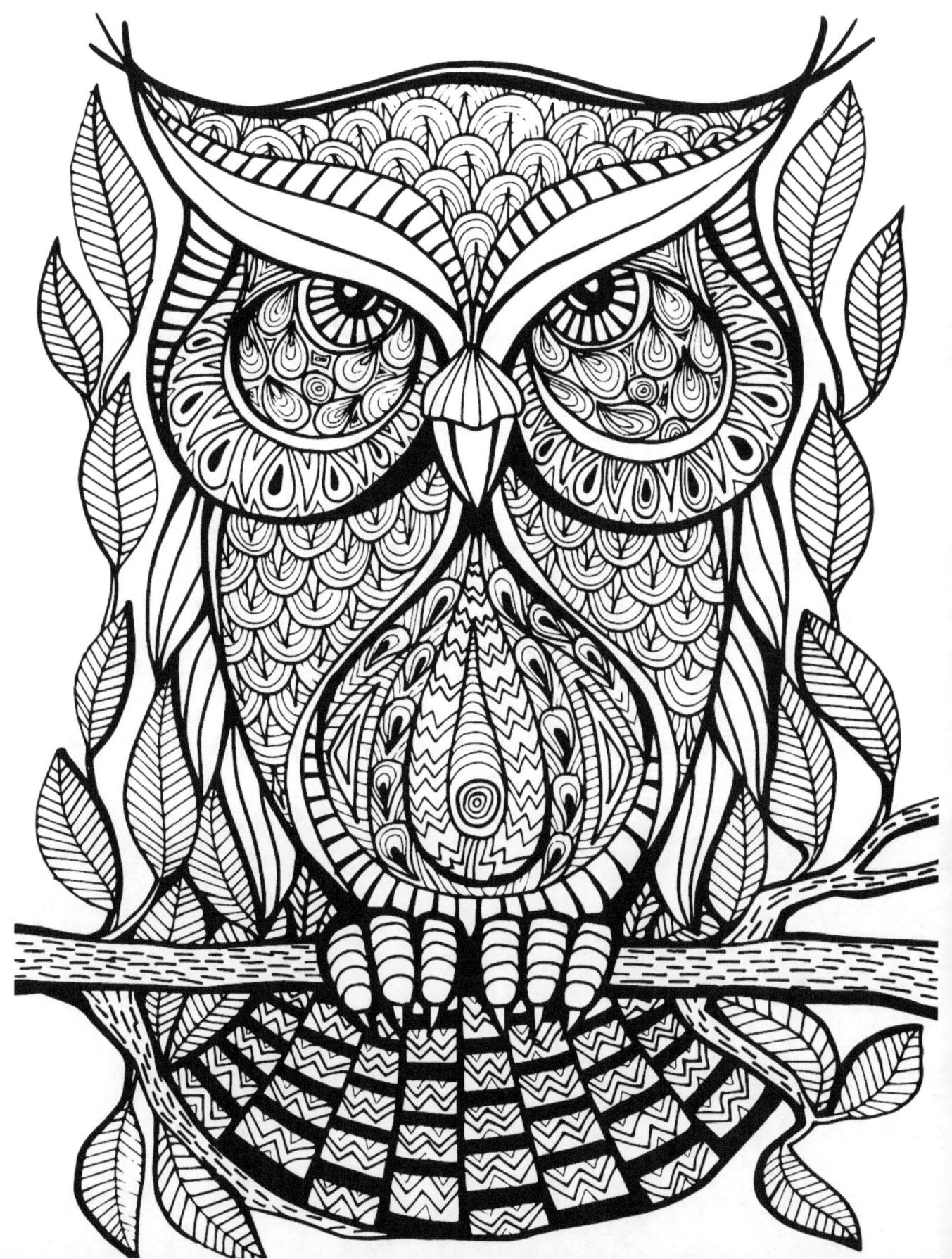

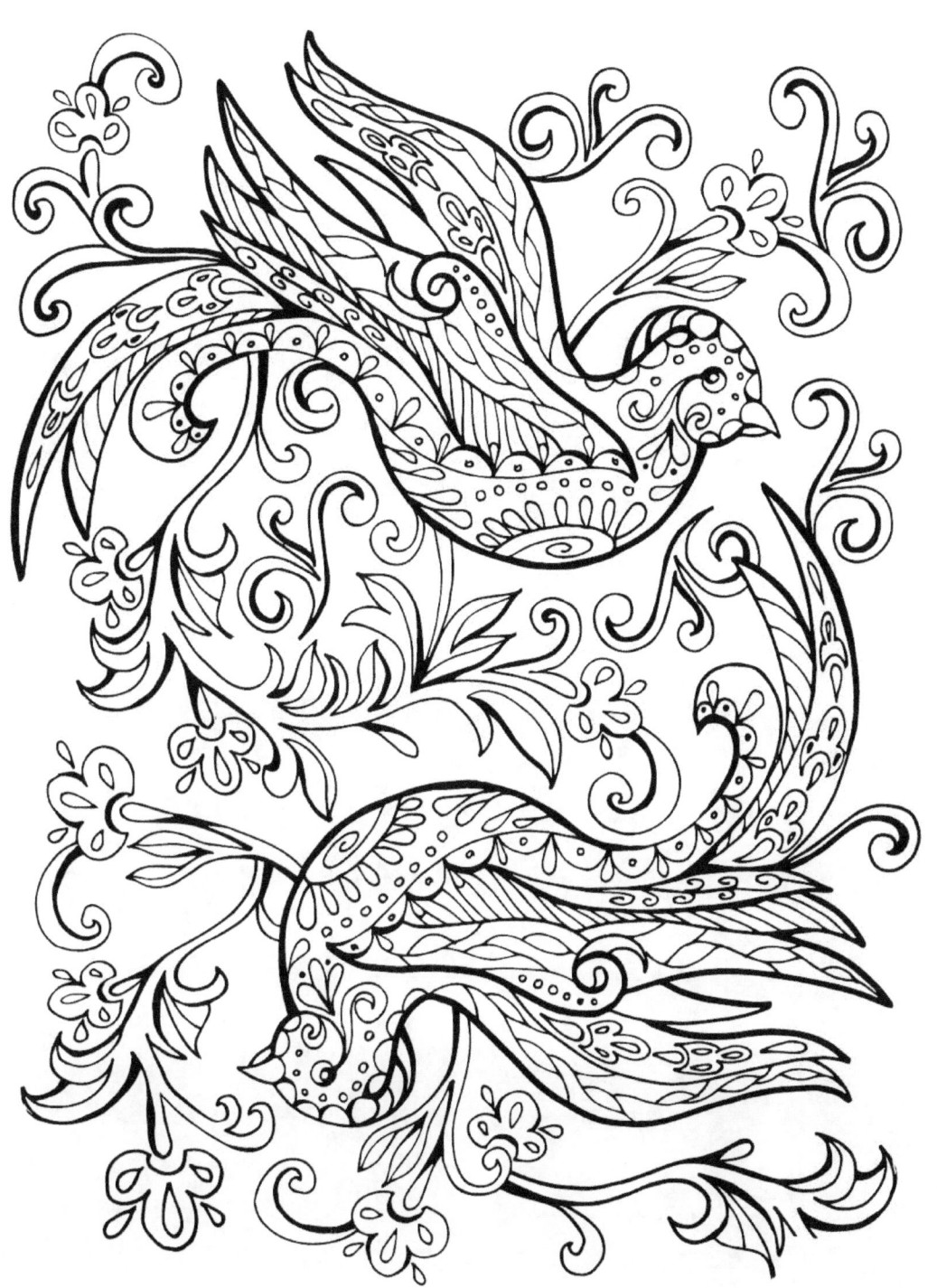

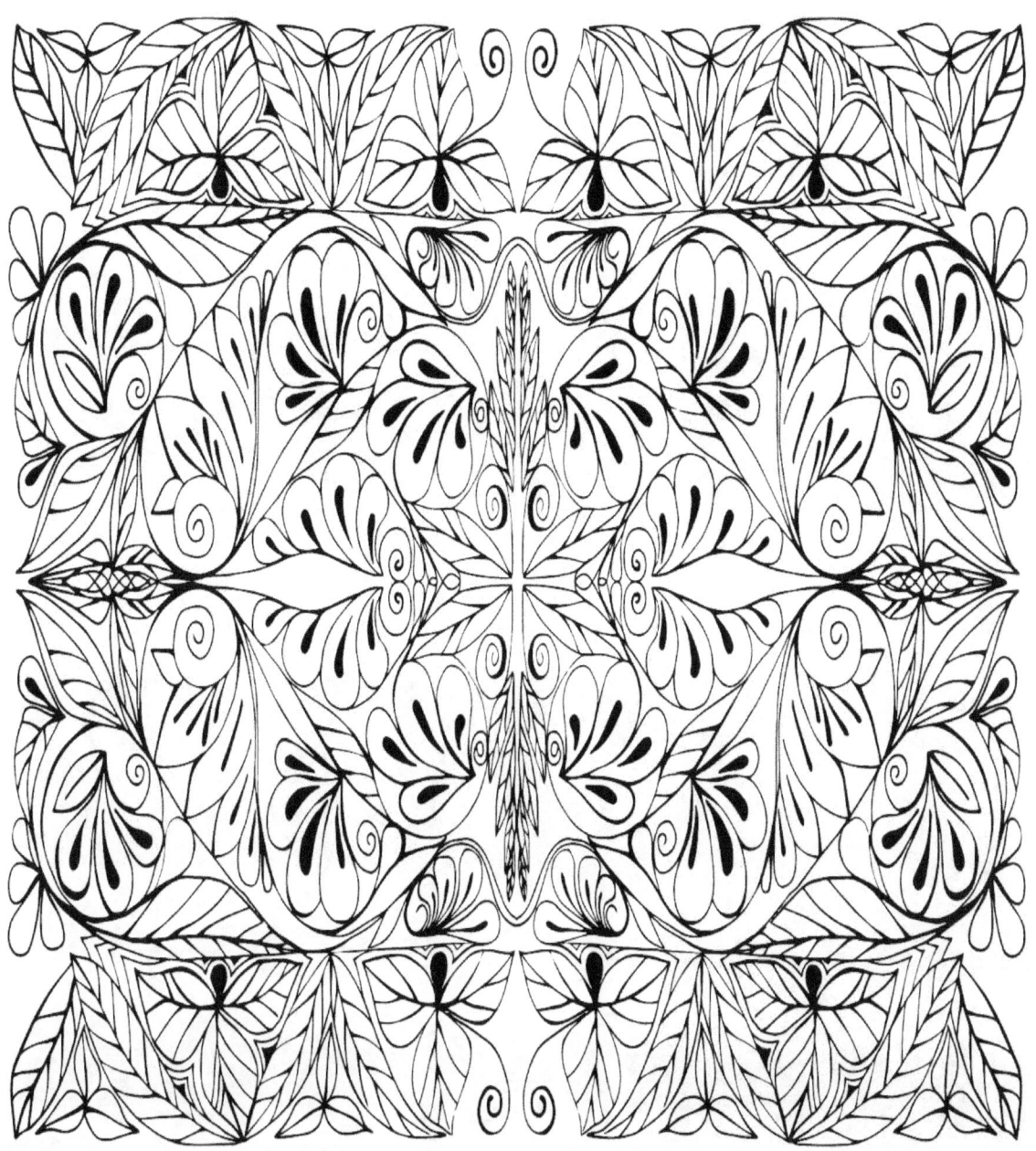

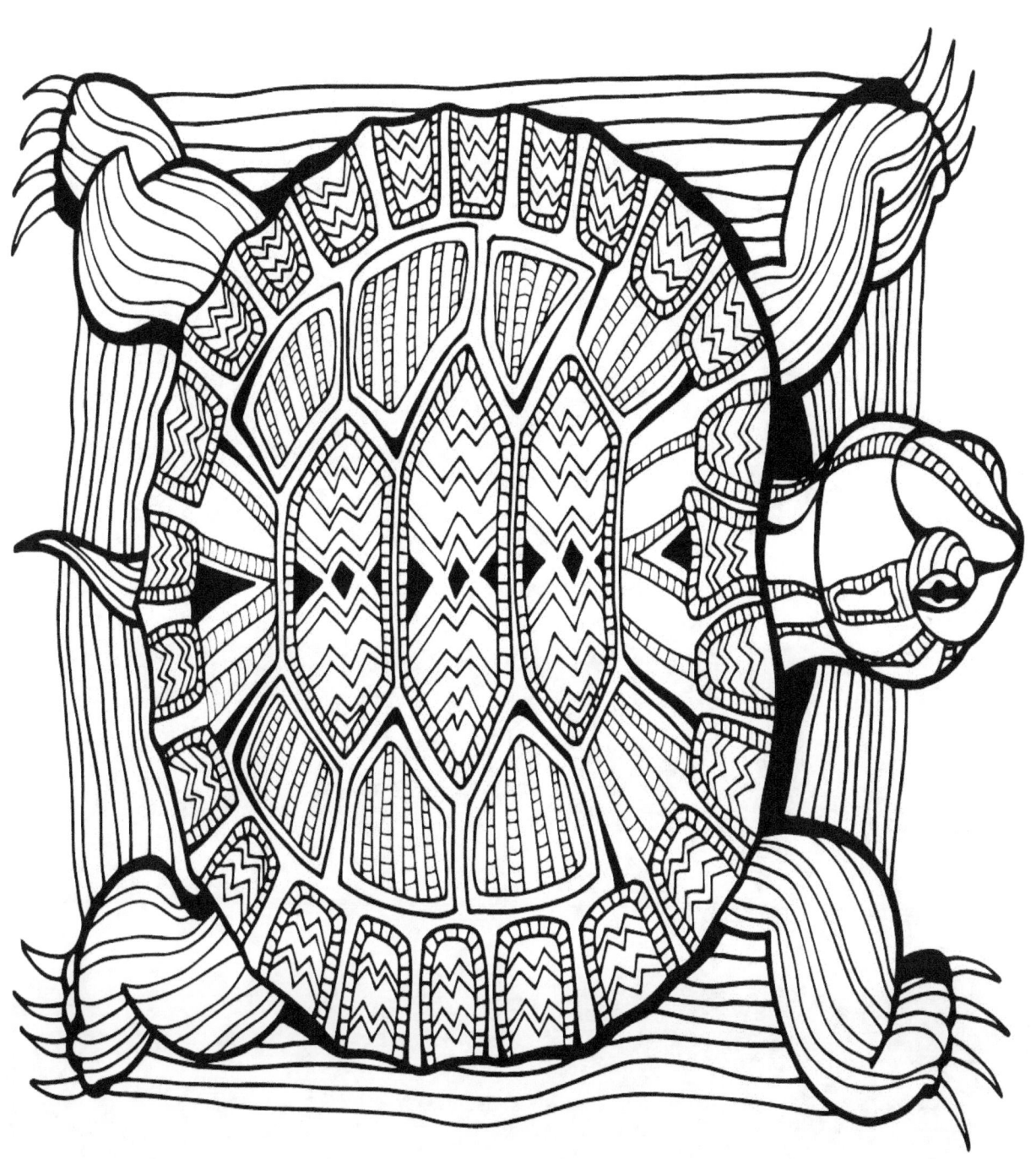

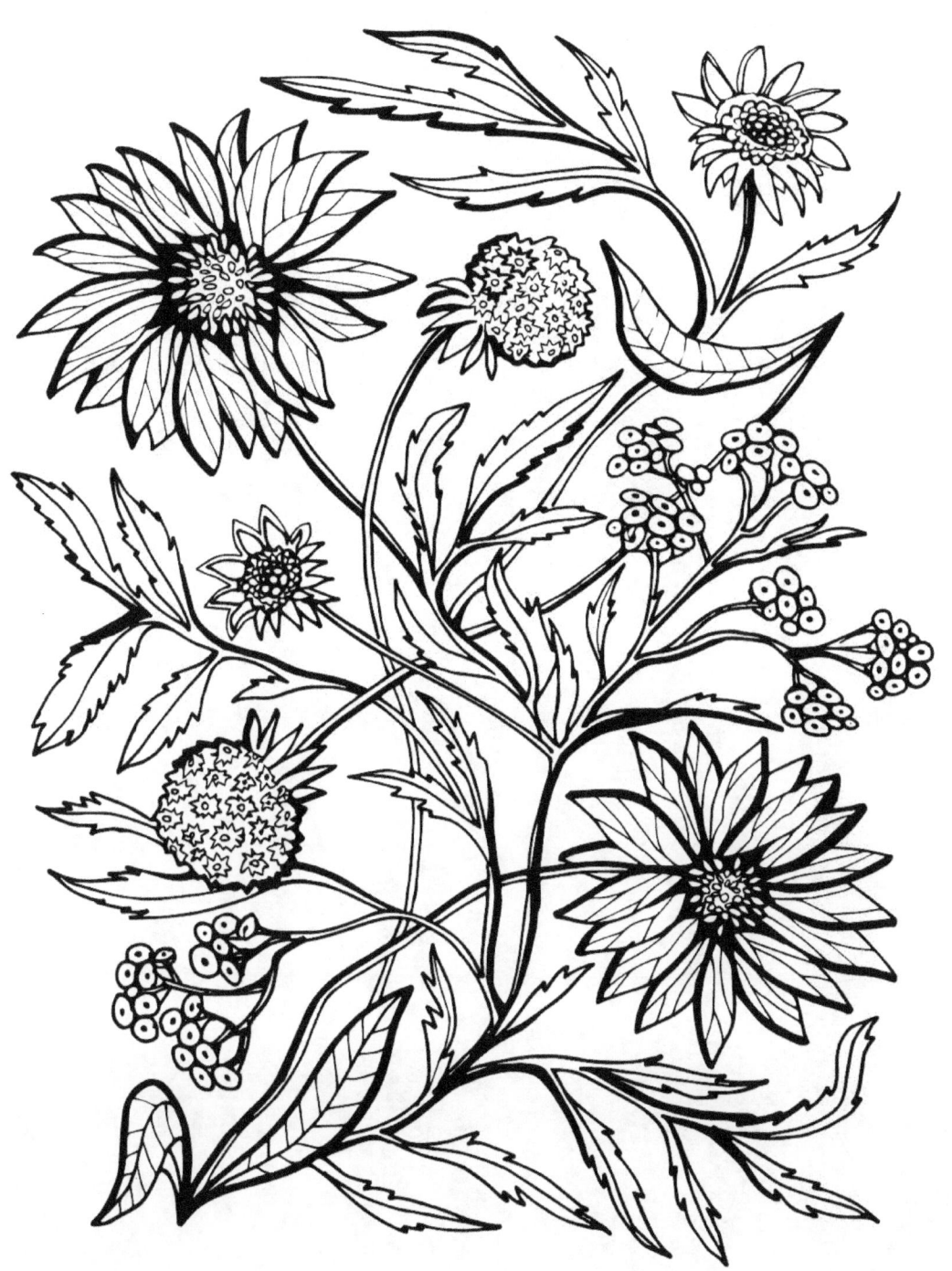

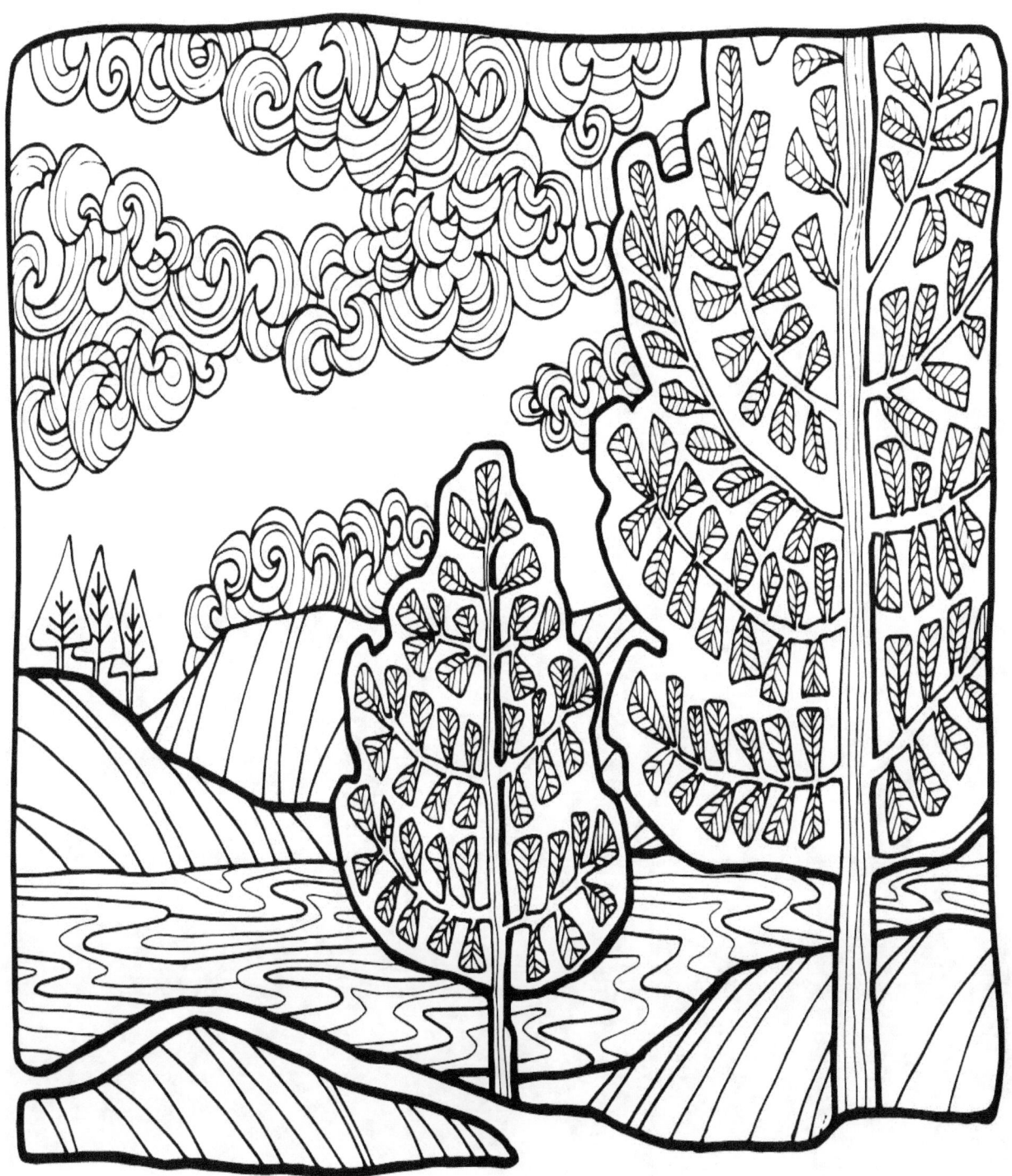

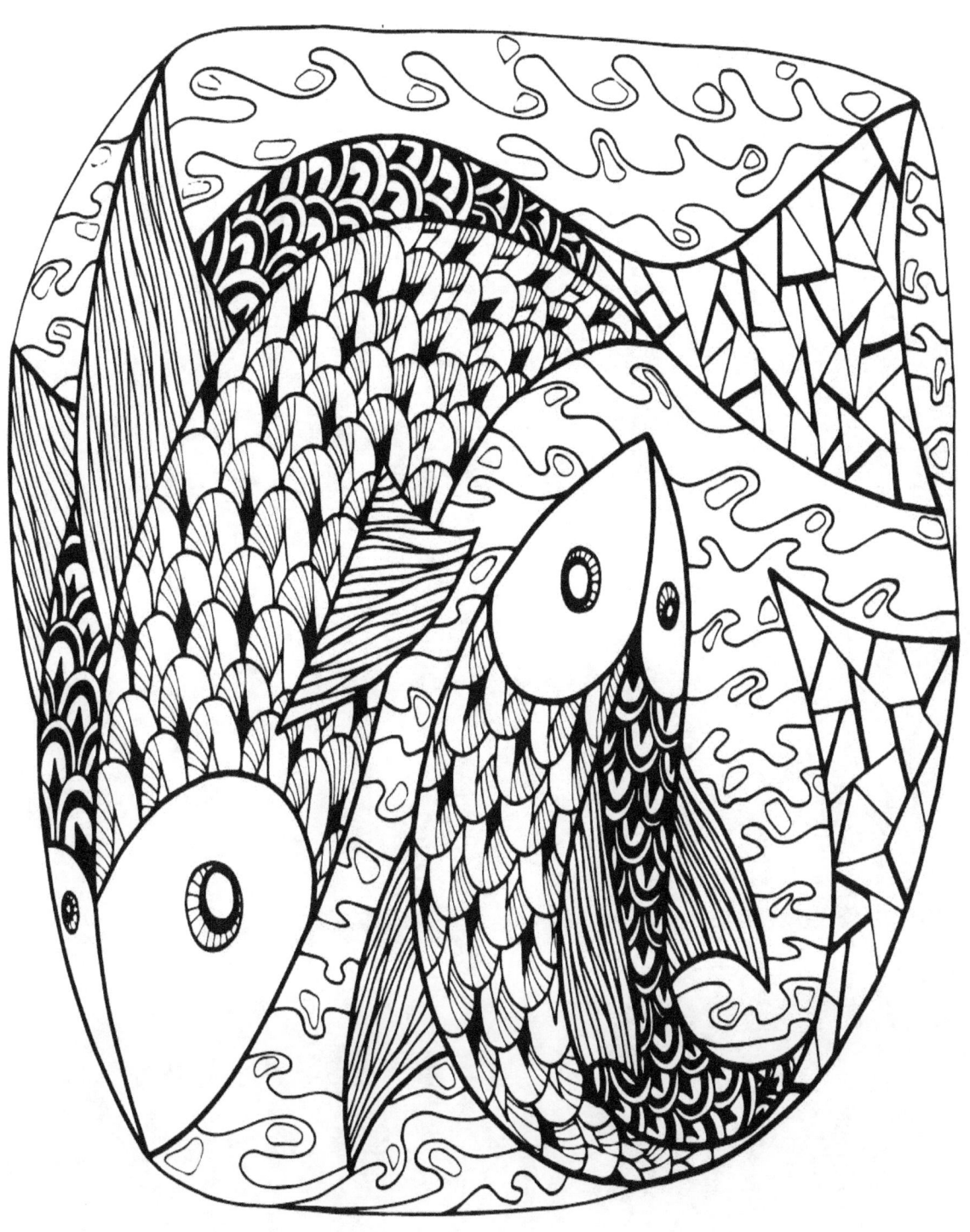

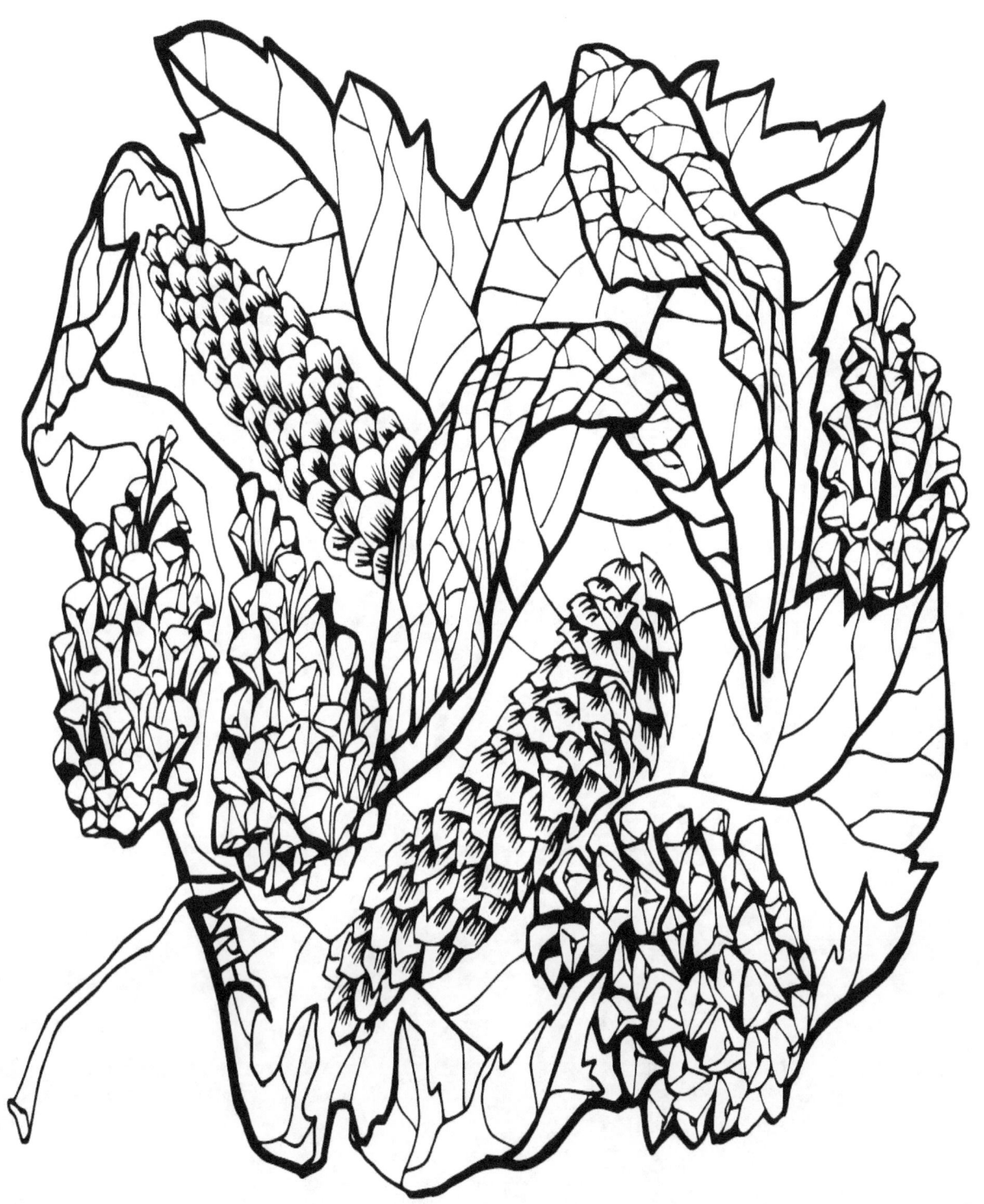

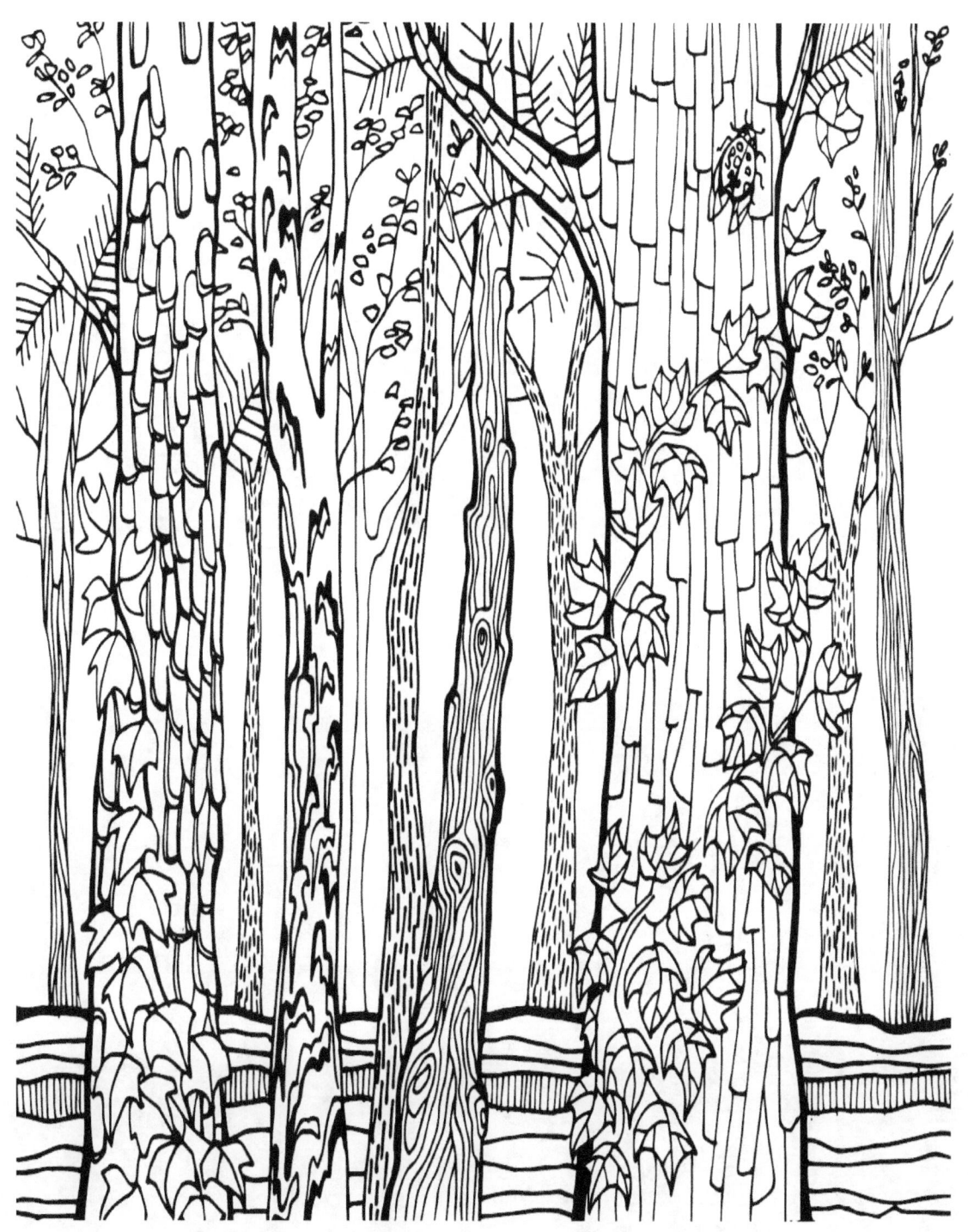

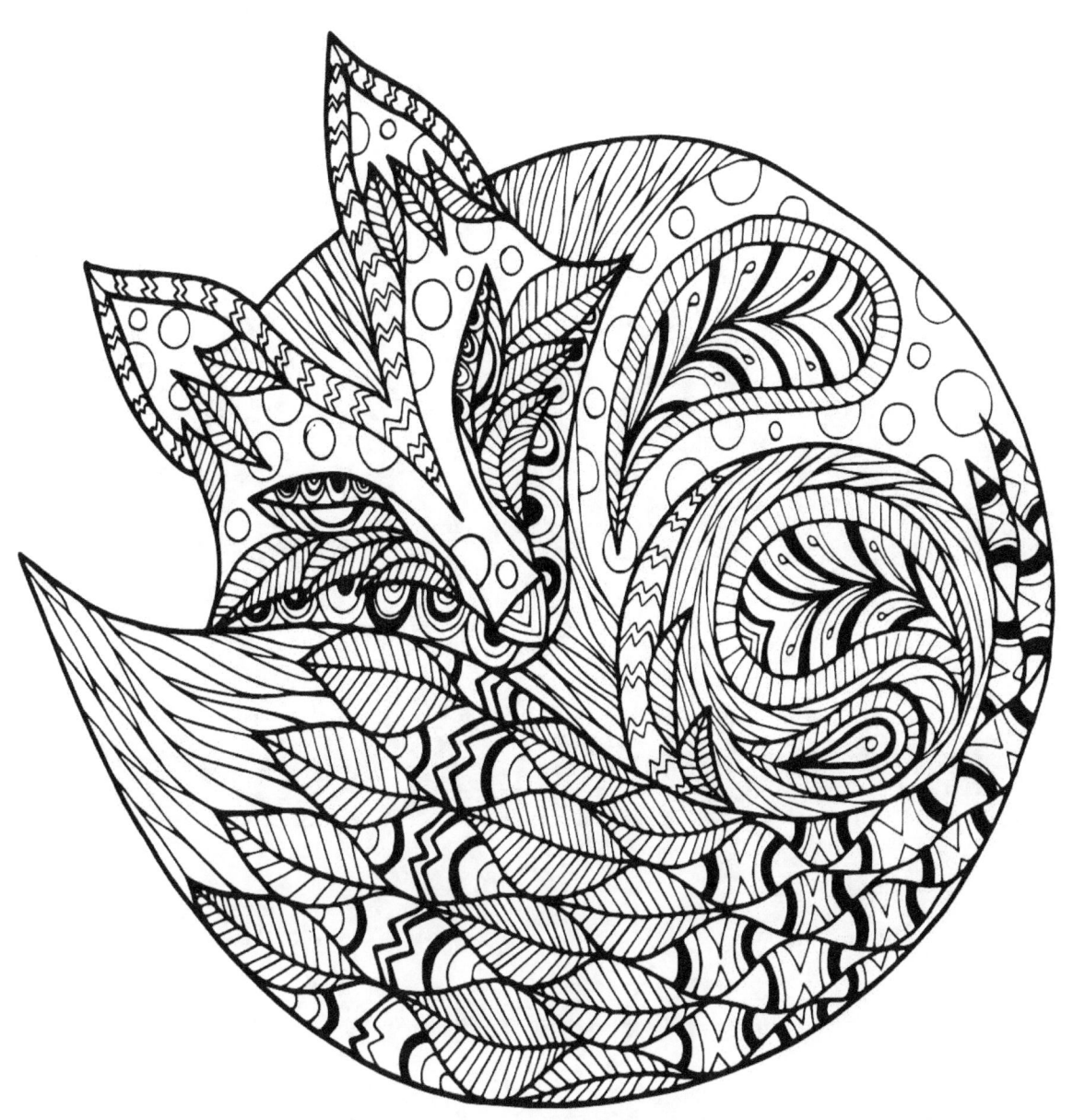

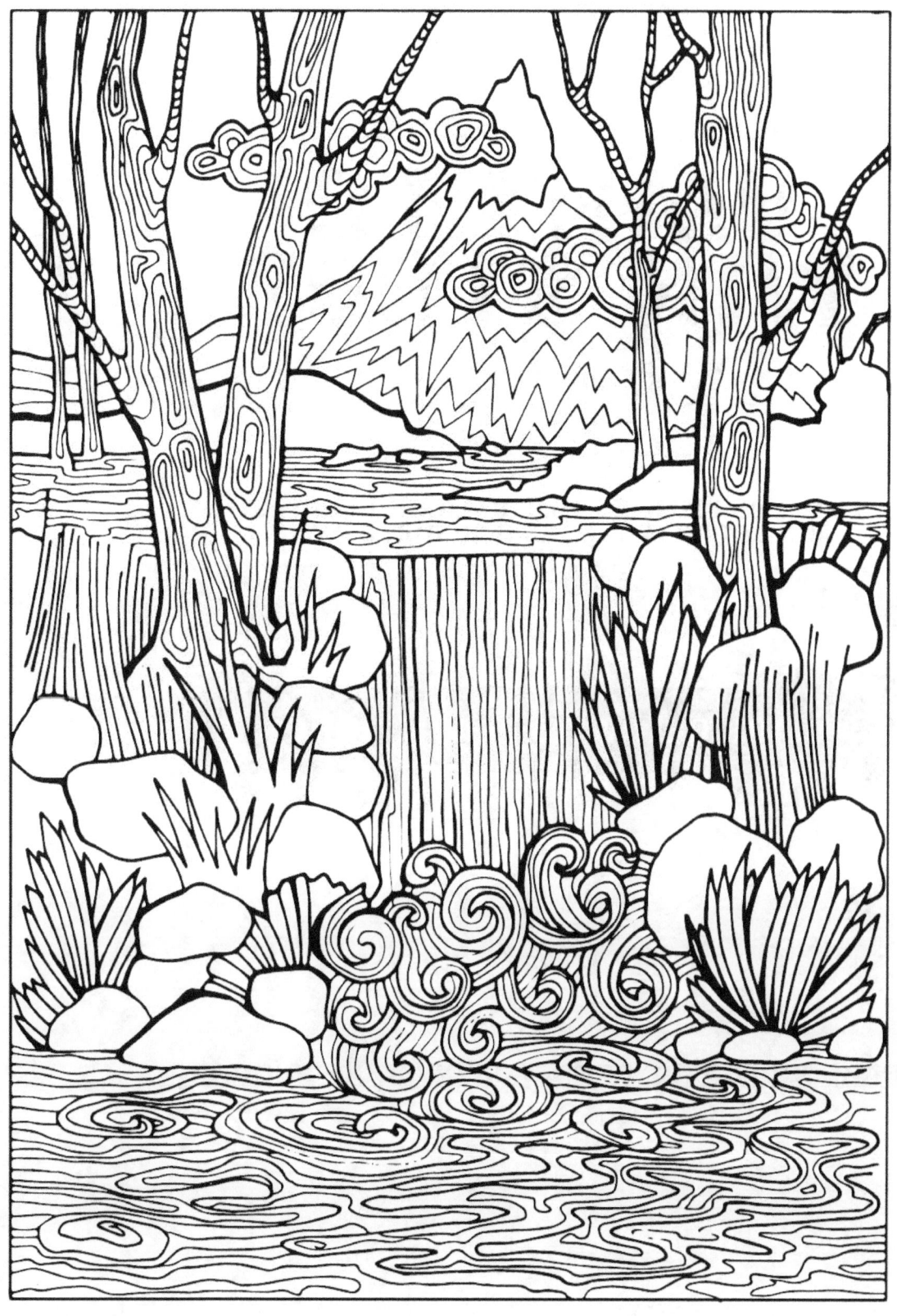

DON'T FORGET TO ENTER THE CONTEST!

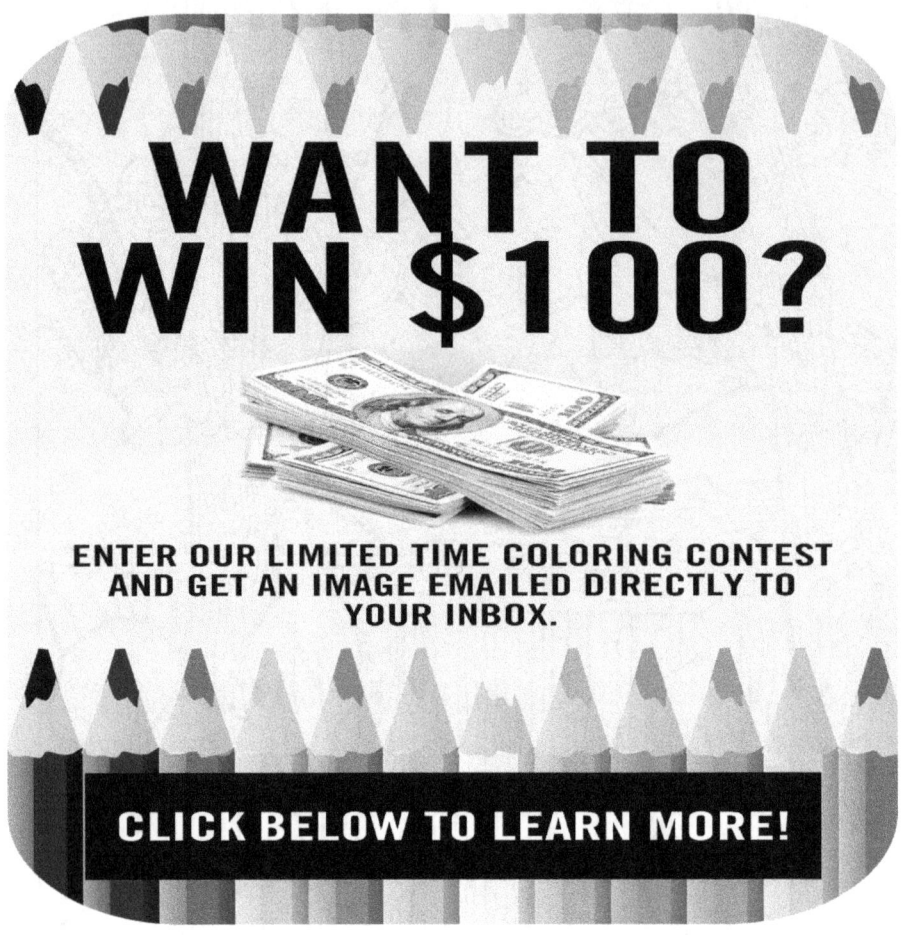

https://zenithpublishing.leadpages.co/adult-colouring-books/

If we want to learn more about us and what we do please check out our "About Us" page on our website, which is totally dedicated to adult coloring books:

http://bestadultcoloringbooks.com/about/

Sincerely,

Katherine & Mary